LET'S VISIT NIGERIA

Let's visit
NIGERIA

NICHOLAS FREVILLE

BURKE

First published October 1968
Second revised edition September 1974
Third revised edition 1985
© Nicholas Freville 1968 and 1974
New material included in this edition © Burke Publishing Company Limited 1985

ACKNOWLEDGEMENTS

The author and publishers are grateful to the following for permission to reproduce photographs in this book:

Colorpix; The Commonwealth Institute; Keystone Press Agency; The Nigerian High Commission; Shell Photographic Services; Spectrum Colour Library and The United Africa Company.

Thanks are also due to Garry Lyle for assistance in the preparation of this edition.

CIP data
Freville, Nicholas
  Let's visit Nigeria – 3rd ed.
  1. Nigeria – Social life and customs – Juvenile Literature
  I. Title
  966.9'05   DT515.4

ISBN 0 222 01041 X

Burke Publishing Company Limited
Pegasus House, 116-120 Golden Lane, London EC1Y 0TL, England.
Burke Publishing (Canada) Limited
Registered Office: 20 Queen Street West, Suite 3000, Box 30, Toronto, Canada M5H 1V5.
Burke Publishing Company Inc.
Registered Office: 333 State Street, PO Box 1740, Bridgeport, Connecticut 06601, U.S.A.
Filmset in Baskerville by Graphiti (Hull) Ltd., Hull, England.
Printed in Singapore by Tien Wah Press (Pte.) Ltd.

85499

Contents

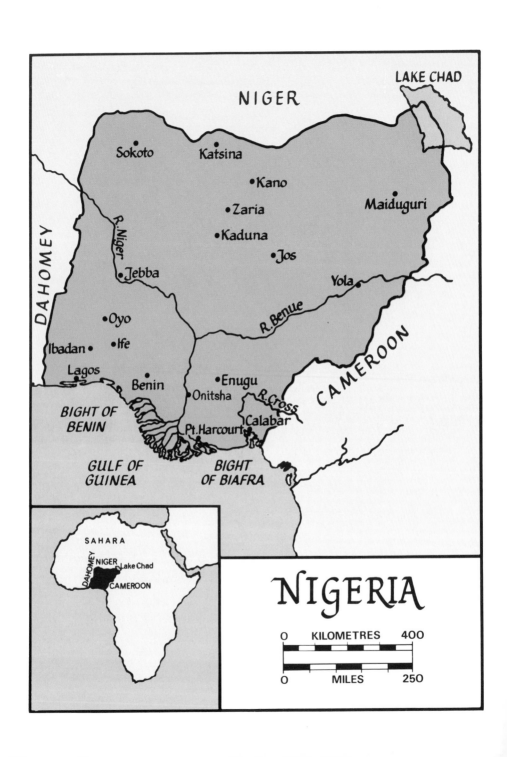

LAKE CHAD

NIGER

Sokoto

Katsina

•Kano

•Zaria

Maiduguri

•Kaduna

R. Niger

•Jos

•Jebba

Yola

DAHOMEY

R. Benue

•Oyo

•Ife

CAMEROON

Ibadan •

Lagos

•Enugu

Benin

•Onitsha

R. Cross

BIGHT OF
BENIN

Calabar

Pt. Harcourt

GULF OF
GUINEA

BIGHT
OF BIAFRA

SAHARA

DAHOMEY

NIGER

Lake Chad

CAMEROON

NIGERIA

0   KILOMETRES   400

0   MILES   250

The Birth of Nigeria

Had I asked my great-grandfather to tell me something about a place called Nigeria in tropical Africa, he would have informed me that there was no such country.

To be sure, he might have known the name Niger; it was the name of a huge river, the longest in West Africa. Many people had heard the name, but very few knew exactly where the river was. A travelling Arab from Tangier had first written about the Niger many hundreds of years ago. As a result, map-makers started decorating their maps of Africa with a new river; on some maps it flowed westwards, on some to the east, on some it got lost in the sands of the Sahara.

In the meantime the merchants and traders of the Mediterranean lands bought shipments of ivory and gold, ebony and other valuable timber, carvings and leather goods. Slowly the news spread that most of these goods came from the land of the big river which ran through the desert. Then it was only a question of time until somebody from the western world "discovered" this fabled country.

A young Scotsman named Mungo Park was the first European to find the river that was to give its name to the country. He was the first to find that the river flowed across from west to east and then down to the south. He must have been a young man of great courage for he went there twice, in 1795 and 1805. In the end he died, with all the members of his expedition, in one of the river's swollen rapids.

It must have been a scene very similar to this that met the eye of the first trader who ventured up-river from the coast

Mungo Park, and the other explorers who followed him to Africa, came from the west or the north. But for many years previously seafarers had visited the Gulf of Guinea, in the "armpit" of Africa. The sailors came to buy slaves whom they took back to work in the plantations of the New World. Portuguese, Spanish, British, French and Dutch sailors knew the Guinea coast. In fact, many of the coastal towns—such as Calabar—were given their names by the captains of the old slave-ships.

The African coast was as rich as the country which lay beyond it. When slave-trading finally came to an end in 1840, as a result of the passing of laws against slavery, trading in goods actually increased. This was partly because a British squadron had been sent to keep the peace in the coastal region known as the Bight of Biafra. What could be more natural than for the traders to sail up the broad river estuaries, and follow the course of the rivers as far as they were navigable?

By the 1860s, many individual traders and companies were competing for trade along the Guinea coast, and making treaties with the neighbouring chiefs. Gradually, one trading company became stronger and more active than all the others. This company was given a royal charter and became known as the Royal Niger Company.

The royal charter was a very important document. It gave the company the right to make treaties with the chiefs, to establish its own police force and to set up courts of law—in other words, to govern the country.

At the end of the nineteenth century, quite a lot was known about the huge river called Niger. The powerful trading company of the same name was well established along the coast to the east and west of the swampy estuary and, of course, up the river. But there was still no mention at that time of a country called Nigeria.

The region was inhabited by many different tribes, such as the Ibos, Ibibios, Tivs and Yorubas. In some of the tribal regions there were highly developed city-states such as Benin and Ife. Further to the north, where the great river turns from the west to the south, there were mighty rulers, called emirs. Some of them ruled empires which were at least a thousand years old. They were warlike and powerful. And, unlike the other Nigerians, they were Muslims. This means that they followed the religion established by Muhammad, the prophet who lived in Arabia in the sixth century A.D. It is thought that the Muslim religion was introduced into this region by Muhammadans in the thirteenth century.

The Royal Niger Company had dealings with all these people, as did the missionaries, teachers and prospectors who followed them to Africa. There were arguments and small-scale wars, and the Europeans found that they needed protection and help.

Finally, much against its will, the British government sent aid. It also sent one of its most outstanding men, F. D. Lugard, who in the early years of the twentieth century created the Crown Colony of Nigeria, and thus united the whole region.

Previously, the country had consisted of several protectorates, where people were governed by foreign rule but were not given full rights of citizenship of the ruling country. By making one colony, the inhabitants were granted the same rights as British citizens.

Nigeria is a vast region of over 921,000 square kilometres (about 356,000 square miles); in it live well over 82 million people, many of whom are as different from one another as, say, a Russian is from a Scotsman.

The task which faced Lugard was enormous. He made treaties, but he also conquered by force when he had to, especially in the north. Finally, he succeeded in creating order and in providing an efficient administration for running the huge country.

Since there were three main groups of people in Nigeria, the

A Hausa from the north of Nigeria

whole area was divided into three regions. The northern half of the country, where the majority of the people live, became the Northern Region. The southern half was divided into the Western and Eastern Regions.

The Northern Region was inhabited by the Hausa, Fulani and Kanuri peoples; the Eastern Region by the Ibos; and the Western Region by the Yorubas. Some time ago, another smaller division was created out of the Western Region, called the Mid-Western Region, where the Itsekeri people lived, to the west of the Niger river.

Each of the regions originally had an internal government for running its own affairs. But it was found that a national government was needed to look after the affairs of the country as a whole. A state capital was therefore created in Lagos, with regional capitals at Kaduna in the north, Enugu in the east, Benin in the mid-west and Ibadan in the west.

As the British occupied the whole area and treated it as one country, many of the native inhabitants began to think in terms of one country—that is, Nigeria. In addition, they realized that in order to be able to do the same work in their own country as the white man was doing, they would have to have the knowledge and education of the white man; otherwise they could not compete with him. The need for education was made clear, throughout the country, in every way.

Nigerians showed ability and skill in learning, and the colonial government and the voluntary societies did their best to help. The result was that by 1958 there was only one white

State House, the official residence of the Head of State in Lagos, the capital of Nigeria at the time of independence

official to every twenty Nigerians in the whole of the federal administration.

In 1960 Nigeria became a fully independent country, a member of the Commonwealth of Nations in her own right, and in 1963 the country was proclaimed the Federal Republic of Nigeria. Let us have a look at independent Nigeria, and at the men who have made her one of the most important and progressive countries in modern Africa.

13

The Making of a Nation

About sixty years ago there was a young Ibo boy fom Eastern Nigeria who was exceptionally intelligent and energetic. As he grew older, he began to travel, he wrote books and articles and, in due course, his name became known. People started enquiring about him. They wanted to know what he thought, and what he advised them to do. In this way, he acquired a large following, not only in his own tribe, but all over the country. His name is Nnamdi Azikiwe, but everybody knows him as "Zik". He became the owner of newspapers, a writer, a banker and, finally, a political leader. He formed his own political party and he called it "The National Council of Nigeria and the Cameroons".

Not unnaturally, the people of the Western and Northern Regions also wished for political representation; so the Yorubas of the Western Region, under the Yoruba chief Awolowo, formed a political party called "Action Group"; and the people from the north, headed by the wealthy and influential Sardauna of Sokoto, established their own party and named it "The Northern People's Congress".

These parties all had one thing in common: they taught people to think of themselves as Nigerians: and they all had

14

The man in the white robes is
Nnamdi Azikiwe ("Zik"), the
first President of Nigeria

Nigerian leaders. All three parties were organized in accordance with the laws of the colony and with the help and advice of the British.

After much argument, the three parties agreed on the new constitution of their country and when, in 1960, the former colony became independent everything was ready. "Zik" became Governor General and, in 1963, the first President of the Republic. Since the President came from the Ibo people in

15

the Eastern Region, Sir Abubakar Tafawa Balewa, a Northerner, was made Prime Minister. He was very much respected, not only in Africa, but all over the world. Chief Awolowo was also given an important post as he was the representative of the Yorubas from the Western Region. In this way, all three main regions were represented in the new administration.

Independence was celebrated with great rejoicing all over Nigeria. Huge bonfires were lit and the feasting, music and dancing lasted for days. Then the government of the new country settled down to work.

They had much to do. There were new roads, railways and airfields to build; schools, training-centres, colleges and hospitals to be established; harbours, mines, wells and mills to be developed.

Meanwhile, factories, banks and transport companies were set up. In addition, oil and large quantities of coal were found near the coast in Eastern Nigeria.

Foreign countries—the United States, Britain, Germany and others—freely helped the young country, lending her money for her needs. Because Nigeria was so rich in natural resources, she could sell more than she bought, and easily repay these loans.

Unfortunately, however, some Nigerian ministers and officials were not as honest as they should have been. Money which should have gone to the country found its way into private pockets; many officials and their families became very wealthy while the rest of the people remained poor.

In the end, the people became so angry that they decided, with the help of the Nigerian army, to make an end of what they called the "thief-men". In January, 1966, they killed and imprisoned many of the leading men and entrusted the government to an Ibo, General Ironsi.

General Ironsi had been trained in England, and he was a very capable officer. As he was an Ibo, he relied mostly on men of his own tribe to help him to create order and govern the country. The result was that the Yorubas from the west and the Muslim Hausas and Fulanis from the Northern Region became jealous. They were afraid of having too many Ibos in the government. In July 1966, they killed Ironsi and started to make life difficult for the Ibos.

There are about eight million Ibos. They are very dark and stocky in appearance. They are clever, eager to learn, hard-working and ambitious. Most of them are Christians. They play an important part, not only in Nigeria, but wherever they go in West Africa, as managers and officials, clerks and merchants.

In many places in the Northern Region the mere presence of Ibo clerks or merchants was enough to start riots. A large number of them were killed and many thousands of them left the north and west in order to return to their homeland in the Eastern Region. It is not surprising to learn that they did not feel very friendly towards the other large tribes in Nigeria, after being hunted through the country, and after General Ironsi was killed in July 1966.

The new head of the Nigerian government was a young officer named Yakubu Gowon. He did his best to come to terms with the Ibos, but the Ibos had had enough. They decided that, with their oil and coal and other natural resources, they could be self-supporting. And so they declared themselves independent of the rest of Nigeria in 1967 and named the Eastern Region the Republic of Biafra, under the leadership of the former governor, Colonel Ojukwu. (Biafra was the old name for the Eastern Region used by the local population before the Europeans came, and the part of the Gulf of Guinea near the Eastern Region, was known for hundreds of years as the Bight of Biafra.)

Federal Nigeria could not accept the Ibos' bid for independence and the Ibos would not accept a federal government over them. So, unfortunately, the two sides began to fight one another. This resulted in a dreadful civil war which lasted a long time and caused many deaths and much hard-

Landscape typical of the Eastern Region, the home of the Ibo people

ship. Finally, in 1970, the Biafrans surrendered and their leader went into exile.

Nigeria is now divided into nineteen states, each with its own parliament. Like the federal parliament and the President of the Republic, state parliaments should be democratically elected every four years. However, the country has again come under military rule. Democratic elections were held in 1983, but soon afterwards the government was forcibly replaced by a council of army, navy and airforce officers.

The chief opponents of the Ibos are the people of what was the Northern Region. There are some 28 million of them and they are mostly Muslims. They are dignified, tall and slim, with straight noses. Many of them do not look like Negroes at all, except for their colouring. When Lord Lugard first came to Africa these people were ruled by their emirs. They had a long history and tradition of which they were very proud. They knew quite a lot about the world in general. Many of them had travelled to Mecca—the holy city to which all Muslims like to make a pilgrimage—and they had traded for many generations with Spain, Italy, Egypt and the North African coast across the Sahara. They dealt in ivory, timber and gold; but their main trade was in slaves.

These northern people have a background and social system which is quite different from that of the southerners. They read and speak a form of Arabic. They breed cattle and horses. In earlier times, when they dealt in slaves, they always

A northern chief with his retainers. The picture shows the difference between these northerners and the rest of the Nigerian people

used to regard any kind of ordinary work as something fit only for slaves or Africans from the south. Their rulers were enormously wealthy and had unlimited power. It is not difficult to understand why they became angry when men from the southern tribes came to their land and started telling them what to do and how to do it.

20

The Tribes of Nigeria

Many Nigerians live in the towns and work in offices and factories, but most of them live in the country. They like to stay near their own tribe and very many of them are small farmers.

There are so many different tribes in Nigeria that the Nigerian radio broadcasts in fifteen different languages. Some of the bigger tribes are so large that we should call them nations—like the Yorubas, for instance.

All the tribes have their own customs and dances, their chiefs and their societies. They have their own gods, too—many of them are not Christians.

Yorubas are friendly and they are very attractive to look at. The men like to dress in a pale blue *agbada*, a long, loose-fitting garment. It is usually embroidered, and reaches below the knee. It has an open neck and the wide sleeves can be

A baby being carried in his mother's *oja*

turned back to the shoulders. The women wear a short blouse and a length of cloth wrapped around them to make a skirt. Over this, round the waist, goes a long, wide piece of cloth, called an *oja*. Mothers often carry their babies in the folds of this cloth. Often one can see a mother shopping or working with her baby happily asleep on her back in the oja.

Yoruba women also wear a turban which is tied in a certain way so that the ends stand up above the head. These turbans are very colourful. One can recognize a Yoruba woman a long way away by the shape of her turban or *gele*.

Yoruba men are tall and slim. Many of the best athletes in Nigeria come from the Yoruba nation. And they make good soldiers.

Yorubas believe that their ancestors came many hundreds of years ago from Egypt. They are very proud of their long history.

Scientists and historians say that many of the Yoruba carvings and sculptures look like Ancient Egyptian carvings. They also think that their method of using bronze in their works of art is the same as that used by the Egyptians, so it is possible that the legend is true.

The members of the various Yoruba clans have always lived in a very organized manner. They settled in districts, centred around a town where the king lived. The king, or chief, was known as the *Oba*, and he ruled his people from his town residence. He had his counsellors, his army, his priests and other officials. Some, like the kings of Ife, Benin and Oyo, became

22

Yoruba women on a festive occasion. Note their distinctive turbans

very powerful rulers because their countries were so well
organized.

The people in the country districts live in square, one-room
houses built of mud-bricks. The floor is beaten earth and there
is one window and a door. The doorstep is raised quite high
above the ground, so that small babies cannot get out and

snakes cannot slide in under the door. In the middle of the room is a stone hearth where the fire is lit for cooking. There is very little furniture: a low stool or two, and a hard bed made of bamboo.

Travelling eastward, and crossing the Niger by the main bridge near Onitsha, one enters the part of Nigeria where most of the inhabitants belong to the Ibo nation. There are other, smaller tribes called the Ibibio, the Tiv and the Efik, who live near the coast.

The Ibos have never had kings or powerful chiefs. Each family likes to live alone and the Ibo villages are also independent of each other.

Ibo people have a great liking for learning. If a student cannot win a scholarship, everybody in the family will work and provide money for his studies. Many Ibo students have gone to universities abroad, their studies paid for by a whole village or a large family.

Whatever an Ibo does, he does well. They are great traders and nothing is too much trouble for them. They live simply, and they make good farmers and careful officials.

Most Ibos are Christian. Those who have studied at university, return as teachers, doctors, priests or lawyers and go to the towns to work.

Both men and women wear an ankle-length "skirt" which is made by wrapping a long piece of cloth round themselves several times and tying the end in a knot. The cloth is very often

Young Ibo girls

dark red in colour and is decorated with different patterns. The knot can be undone, and the last round of the "skirt" pulled up to cover the shoulders.

Women and girls wear head-scarves. These are always brightly coloured, but much simpler than the Yoruba turbans.

The Ibo farmer builds himself a very simple house. As this area has more rain than other parts of Nigeria, he does not use nails or wire because these would rust away. Instead, he makes a frame of wood and the wooden posts are woven together with creepers which he can find in the forest. When this "basket-house" is ready, he plasters it with clay and covers the roof with banana leaves.

The Ibo houses are small and square and are very easy to

25

repair. They have no windows, just a door. When the farmer makes more money, he builds stronger houses and uses corrugated iron for roofing.

In the north of Nigeria live the Hausas and the Fulanis and, in the north-eastern corner, the Kanuris. As we have already seen, all these tribes have been converted to the Muslim religion.

In the past the Hausas were a fierce and warlike nation. They lived under the rule of the emirs, whose word was law. The men were mainly occupied in fighting, raiding and trading. All the everyday work was done by the women and the slaves.

The Hausa people are not quite as dark as the people living in the southern half of Nigeria. The men dress in long white flowing robes and wear a white turban. Sometimes they wear a dark embroidered cloak over their white robes. The women prefer dark blue or black robes. They wear a covering on the head which can be pulled over to hide the face. Muslim women do not like their faces to be seen by strangers.

Hausas prefer to live in towns. Many of their towns have some fine old buildings, with walls of decorated clay or plaster and beautifully carved doors.

At home, they like to sit on carpets and cushions or on pieces of sheepskin rather than on chairs or stools.

The Hausas are great traders, and many of them travel not only in Nigeria but all over Africa. They enjoy bargaining and will spend a long time haggling over the price of some article;

but once a Hausa merchant agrees to something, he will keep his word.

In the rural areas, a Hausa or Fulani village can easily be recognized because all the houses are round. The walls are built of clay, and the roofs are thatched and rise to a point like a cone. There is one door, which is so small that you have to bend low to get in and out, and no windows. Men and women live in separate houses.

The largest tribe after the Hausas is the Fulani tribe. The Fulanis, like the Hausas, have a long history. A hundred years ago, they had a very famous ruler, who decided that all the people as far as the Yoruba country should become Muslim. His name was Usuman Dan Fodio. He created a powerful kingdom in northern Nigeria and waged war against all non-Muslims in the south.

Fulani herdsmen and their flock

The Fulani dress is much simpler than that of the Hausas. It is a long, straight robe, often pale yellow or pale blue. The men wear a small skull-cap and, on important occasions, an embroidered cloak. The women wear a dark dress and sometimes as many as six or eight large earrings. The men shave their heads but the women tie their hair into tight plaits.

The Fulanis are cattle-breeders. In very hot weather the herdsmen wear sun-helmets. These are made of straw, often

Fulani cattle being ferried across the Benue river. Note the strange-looking hump and the widespread horns

edged with leather, and shaped like a basket or an upside-down beehive.

Both the Fulanis and the Hausas love horses and take great care of them. Their saddles and bridles are carefully decorated.

The Kanuri is a much smaller tribe. They live in the north-eastern part of Nigeria, called Bornu. The Kanuris, like the Fulanis, are cattle breeders and they are skilful herdsmen. Their main market town is Maiduguri where they sell their animals as well as many thousands of hides. The cattle have huge horns set wide apart, and they have a hump where the neck and the back meet. Most of the cattle are red-brown, but there is also a bigger, grey-coloured breed.

In north-eastern Nigeria there is a small tribe—related to the Fulani—which does not live in any one spot. These are the Mbororos, who move about from place to place, stopping wherever there is enough grass for their cattle to graze on. They wander from Lake Chad in the north-east right down to the south. Their herdsmen use small bows and very dangerous arrows, but they are friendly and kind to other travellers.

There is one other group of people in Nigeria which is not called by the name of a tribe but by the place where they live. These are the "creek people" who live near the sea in the river estuaries, swamps, lagoons and other waterways. They are excellent boatmen and fishermen. The children can swim before they can walk.

The houses of the creek people are built on stilts, right on the

Boats moored on the bank of a creek village

waterline, so they can step straight into their boats and go fishing. The houses are built of mangrove wood, which does not rot in water. The boats used to be made of the trunks of huge trees and the first traders and explorers travelled in these, rowed by eight or more oarsmen with short paddles.

Rivers Between the Sands and the Sea

If you look at the small inset map in the front of this book showing the whole of Africa you will see that Nigeria lies south of the Sahara, between the Sahara and the sea.

Two major rivers flow through Nigeria: the Niger, from the west, and the Benue, from the east. The two rivers meet in the middle of the country and turn south, forming a giant Y.

East and west of the trunk of the giant Y, the country is

31

relatively flat; further north, where the rivers separate, the country becomes steeper and more hilly. In this area, which is called the Bauchi highlands or plateau, there are mountains of over 1,200 metres (4,000 feet).

Nigeria is very near the Equator, and this means that there is no winter or summer. Instead, there is a rainy season, which starts in May and lasts until October, and a dry season. In the far north near the Sahara there is little rain. The nearer we go towards the sea, the heavier the rainfall.

The temperature in the southern part of Nigeria is always about 27 degrees Centigrade (80 degrees Fahrenheit), but the air is very humid and people soon feel tired. In the northern part it can be as hot as 43 degrees Centigrade (110 degrees Fahrenheit) and as cool as 19 degrees Centigrade (67 degrees Fahrenheit) but it is dry and one can sleep well at night.

Most vegetation grows best in a climate which is hot and wet, and this applies equally in Nigeria. In the southern part of the country there are huge forests, extending inland for great distances. Further to the north the forests become thinner and the country has the appearance of an enormous park. Still further north, where the climate is hot and dry, fewer trees are seen; and as one approaches the Sahara there are more and more bushes and shrubs growing in coarse grass, and fewer trees; this kind of land is called *savannah*. North of the savannah country, the only vegetation is rough grass, and beyond that lies the desert.

The Niger and the Benue, and the Cross river in the extreme

32

Landscape typical of northern Nigeria

south-east, bring water to many parts of Nigeria. By the end of
the rainy season, however, these rivers are in flood. Often
bridges are washed away and the flood-waters tear out huge
chunks of earth. Heavy trees float in the rivers and are a danger
to steamers or boats. So much water comes down that when the
river reaches the flat land near the sea, one river-bed is not
enough. The flood-waters spread over the surrounding
countryside and create new channels. That is why the Niger

33

A mangrove swamp. The thick, twisted roots of the mangrove trees can be seen on the right of the picture

has thirteen mouths opening into the sea and the Cross river is simply lost amongst its many outlets.

The land surrounding these estuaries is swampy and is criss-crossed by waterways and channels, known as creeks. The banks of the creeks are lined with mangrove trees. Each tree forms hundreds of thick, twisted roots above the water and these roots go far down into the wet ground. They grow so thickly that it is very hard to cut a way through them.

Where the swamp ends, the forest begins. Some of the trees—such as the iroko, sapele and obeche—provide very valuable timber, which is used for furniture-making. Bamboo, which is used for many purposes, also grows in profusion. There are creepers and climbing plants hanging everywhere. Tree-trunks are covered in shiny green moss. There are palm trees of all sorts, many ferns and some beautiful orchids. Every now and then one comes across a lovely tree, with clusters of bright red flowers, called Flame-of-the-Forest.

Vegetation grows so quickly in the forests that an unused clearing will be overgrown in a few months' time.

There are not many animals here because there is not enough food for them, but in the morning and evening the air is filled with the noise of millions of crickets. Occasionally one comes across a very small antelope, no bigger than a cat. But most of the animals live high up in the tops of trees: chattering little grey monkeys and a variety of birds of the hornbill family. There are very few snakes, and those that there are, are mainly harmless.

Beyond the rain-forests, and in northern Nigeria, the inhabitants go hunting. Hunting is done with the help of dogs. These Nigerian hunting-dogs cannot bark. They are smooth-haired and are about as big as a terrier. Nigerians call them "pie" dogs. Each one has a little wooden bell round its neck which makes a musical sound. The owner of the dog can recognize the sound of his bell and will know where to go to. In many places, especially in the north, many hunters still use spears. Others use muzzle-loading guns with very long barrels, some of which actually have to be held steady by one man while another is firing it.

In the Bauchi highlands there are many baboons. These big monkeys with their dog-like faces move about in large troops. Their biggest enemy is not man but the leopard, a beautiful and very dangerous animal which roams around in this region.

Near the Sahara there are antelope and deer. These are always on the move searching for grass to eat and water to drink.

There are snakes in the drier parts of Nigeria. Some are poisonous and dangerous, although they will not attack people unless they are frightened. There are vultures and hyenas, too.

Vultures and hyenas are not likable animals, but they do very useful work. When an animal dies in the bush, or a sheep or a goat is lost from the herd, the vultures and hyenas clear away the carcass. Hyenas do not show themselves in daylight, but they will approach a village at night, and can be heard howling and "laughing".

Lagos and Other Towns

In the middle of the Bight of Benin, in the Gulf of Guinea, a narrow channel from the sea leads into a lagoon. On an island in that lagoon, five hundred years ago, Portuguese sailors found a little village; and that is how Lagos—until very recently the official capital of Nigeria—was discovered.

In those days, the entire area was a giant swamp. Its mosquitoes, damp heat and tropical diseases gave it the name "white man's grave". But this did not prevent it from becoming one of the main centres of the slave trade, with the powerful African chiefs capturing the weaker tribes and selling them to the slave-traders.

In the middle of the nineteenth century, the British Navy was given orders to remove the slavers from the Bight of Benin. In 1861 the powerful king of Lagos agreed to stop raiding for slaves; in return, the British gave him a thousand bags of cowrie shells, which represented a good deal of wealth. He handed over Lagos to the British, and from that day Lagos began to grow in peace.

One of the many
modern buildings
in Lagos

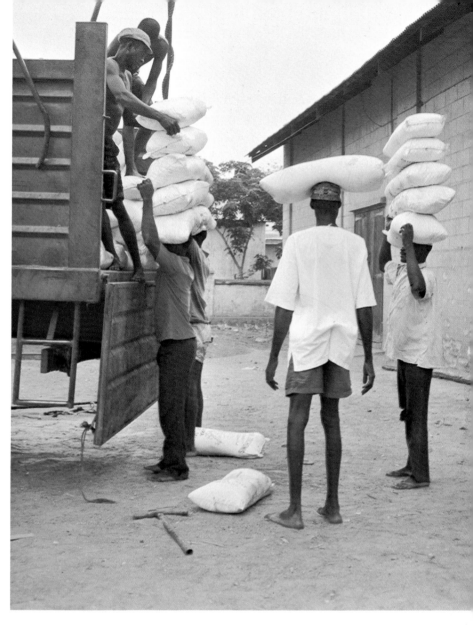

Whatever the burden it is likely to be carried on the head. These men are carrying sacks of salt in Kano

Today, Lagos is a thriving and progressive city. There was electric street-lighting in Lagos before there was any in London. The roads are paved and there are banks, shops, offices, schools, hospitals and everything else that a modern city needs.

Lagos has grown so much that the island is not large enough for the 1,500,000 inhabitants. Although the suburbs are on the mainland, many of the big government offices are on the neighbouring islands, and are connected by bridges.

A view of Lagos

One of Lagos's main streets has hundreds of small, open-fronted shops, where a great variety of goods are displayed for sale. Nigerians are very fond of colourful clothes and in these small shops one can find silks, velvets and cotton materials. Some of these cottons have rather odd designs printed on them—the letters of the alphabet, for instance, or a picture of a telephone, or even the prime minister's face.

Among the laden lorries and carts which weave their way through the streets can be seen men with huge parcels on their heads. Loads are always carried on the head, however large or heavy they may be. School-children carry their books in the same way, and they can run, play games and even fight without the books falling off.

Lagos is one of the major sea-ports of Africa and over half of the sea-borne trade of Nigeria goes through the port, which continues to grow.

It is not a very long train journey from Lagos to the capital of the Western State. This is Ibadan, the second largest city in Nigeria with nearly one million inhabitants.

Everyone in Nigeria is very proud of Ibadan, which has one of the best universities in Africa. Students come there from all over the English-speaking world. For many years, most of the teachers came from the University of London, but now there are many Nigerian professors lecturing at the place where they were once students themselves.

The university is not very far from the town, which is sur-

A bird's-eye view of the old city of Kano. Its strangely shaped houses are made of dried clay

rounded by low hills. The buildings are white and airy and from a distance they look as if they had been cut out with a fretsaw.

Far away, to the north of Nigeria, is the famous city of Kano the capital of the state of the same name.

This ancient city is quite different from the other main towns or cities of Nigeria. The houses are made of dried clay and have flat roofs, because there is never much rain. The whole town is surrounded by an immense high wall, with thirteen gates in it. In the midst of the brown houses, rise the two tall, slender turrets of the gleaming white Muslim church —the huge mosque of Kano.

Outside the ancient walled city is the modern town with its factories, shops and houses. Near by is Kano Airport where a trumpeter of the Emir of Kano, sitting on a white racing camel, once used to salute the long-distance jets.

Kano is the town of the Hausas and is the biggest town on the southern edge of the Sahara. It was from here that the caravans set out across the Sahara with slaves, ivory and gold. Even now there are quite a few camels to be seen.

Because it is on the edge of the desert, there is much dust in this region. For two whole months, the wind blows from the Sahara and the dust makes the air look foggy. This desert wind

A modern factory in Enugu

The beautiful gleaming-white mosque of Kano where the inhabitants are followers of the Muslim religion

is called the *harmattan*. When it blows, the men pull the loose fold in their turbans over their faces to protect themselves against the dust.

The capital of the East Central State is Enugu. It looks very different from Kano, with its wide avenues, squares and many trees. Coal is mined near the city.

Not far from Enugu is Onitsha, which has a beautiful new cathedral and the biggest market in the whole of West Africa.

The new cathedral at Onitsha. Most of the people of the East Central State are Christian

There are other important towns in Nigeria, among them Kaduna, the capital of the North Central State; Bonny, on the coast; and Port Harcourt, the second largest port in the country.

45

Tribal Chiefs and Customs

Before the Europeans came to Nigeria, the inhabitants lived under the rule of their kings, emirs and other chiefs. Some of these kings had great power and had many lesser chiefs under them. The Emir of Kano and the Oni of Ife were looked upon as the greatest of rulers.

As we have seen, when Nigeria became independent, she was

no longer ruled by tribal chiefs and kings but by a government of ministers. At first this was difficult for many Nigerians to accept. So to make government easier, it was arranged in each region that the ministers should have a council to help them. This council was made up of all the tribal chiefs and was called the House of Chiefs.

The chiefs no longer made the rules and laws, but they advised the government about the laws and customs of their own tribes. The kings and chiefs are held in great respect, even by the members of the government.

The kings of the various tribes of the Yoruba nation all accept the Oba of Ife as the chief king. He is known as the Oni and he is the keeper of all the sacred objects of the Yorubas. When a new Oba, or king, is crowned in one of the smaller Yoruba tribes, he is crowned by the Oni of Ife.

The Obas of the Yoruba tribes have their own titles. For example, the Oba of Oyo is called the Alafin, the Oba of Abeokuta is the Alake, the Oba of Warri is the Olu. These titles all have meanings, such as "the crocodile who devours his enemies", or "the elephant who destroys his opponents". They were invented long ago to frighten enemy tribes.

When one of the Obas goes anywhere, it is an occasion for great pomp and display. The Oba is dressed in a beautiful embroidered gown and his slippers are decorated with gold and silver. He wears a golden crown and often he carries a long elaborately decorated staff. His servants bear his sword and stool. Around him are his officials and friends, all dressed in

An Oba, or chief, dressed in ceremonial robes. Note the gold crown and umbrella of state

flowing robes. A number of drummers go before him and herald his coming by beating their drums. Immediately behind the Oba walks a servant holding a huge umbrella of state over him. This umbrella is coloured and decorated and bears the golden badge—or crest—of the Oba: an elephant, perhaps, or a crocodile, or a tortoise.

The Obas and the lesser chiefs have many duties to perform.

For instance they are the custodians of the land, which belongs to the whole tribe and not to individuals. It is they who make sure that each farmer has a piece of land on which he can raise crops. It is they who give permission for valuable trees to be

A meeting in progress beneath the shade of a leafy tree

felled and sold for timber. The chiefs also act as judges for their particular district in the many quarrels and fights which occur in the villages.

The kings and chiefs have their own councils. These are made up of the older men of the tribe. An important chief like the Oni of Ife has his own palace and council chamber. A small tribe can hold a council in the open under the shade of a tree.

The Ibos have no big chiefs. Their place is taken by the elders of the village.

The emirs of northern Nigeria are still much respected. They do not wage war any longer nor do they make laws, but all their people acknowledge their importance. For many hundreds of years, they have been wealthy and have exercized great authority. Four hundred years ago, when Emir Mousa went on a pilgrimage to Mecca—where the prophet Mohammed was born—it took a thousand camels to carry his gold.

The emirs held court in their cities. They were surrounded by merchants, travellers, musicians and many learned men. These learned men were lawyers, doctors, writers and teachers; they all spoke Arabic and followed the Arab way of life. Each of the emirs had a vast army, chiefly of cavalry, who were armed with swords and spears.

One of the most powerful of emirs was the ruler of Sokoto in north-western Nigeria. He was so great that he was not called emir, but was given the title of sultan. He was not only a powerful chief, but also the head of all Muslims in Nigeria, and he directed the religious ceremonies.

The present ruler of Sokoto still has a mounted body-guard and on great occasions hundreds of his people follow him on horseback. When he wishes to entertain his visitors he lines up his horsemen in the distance. Then, at a given signal, they start galloping towards the spectators. In flowing white robes, sabres drawn, lances set, and shouting their war-cries, hundreds of horsemen come thundering straight at the visitors. When they are only a short distance away, they suddenly pull up their rearing horses. There is a cloud of dust and a great swirl of horses and men. Then the wonderful display is over. There is no sight like this anywhere else in the world.

The Emir of Daura (centre), one of Nigeria's tribal leaders

When we think of a family, we usually mean a father, mother and children. But in Nigeria, a family means all the people who are related.

A Nigerian household will consist of a father and mother and their children, and all the uncles, aunts, cousins and other relatives who wish to live with them. The head of the household is the man who is able to feed and generally look after this large family. Even a Nigerian who has studied abroad and returns home as a qualified accountant or lawyer or teacher has to look after all his relatives, not only his own wife and children. He still feels bound by the old tribal customs.

When the Europeans came to Nigeria, they encountered people whom they called witch-doctors. In fact, these people were neither witches nor doctors. Some believed in human sacrifice, and did much harm; but many were simply pagan priests. There were others who claimed they could make rain or prevent storms and floods, or that they had the power to foretell the future. All of them knew about medicine. They treated wounds and tried to heal the sick. They learned about the different plants and herbs of the forests and how to use them. There were many illnesses they could cure.

In parts of Nigeria today there are native doctors. They know a great deal about useful plants and herbs. In the Nigerian universities scientists and doctors are very interested to learn from the native doctors. These people no longer cast bones and sacrifice chickens but try to do their work honestly.

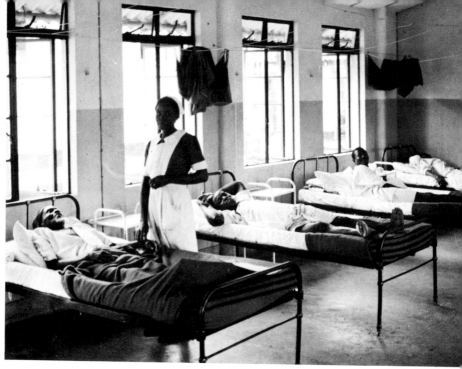

At one time these people would have gone to the witch-doctor for a cure for their sickness. Now more and more people come to hospitals like this one for treatment

Often they advise the sufferer to go to one of the big hospitals to see a qualified doctor.

Perhaps the nicest custom in Nigeria is the hospitality the people offer to strangers. Not only in the towns but also in the poorest village a stranger will be offered something to eat and drink. The people are friendly, kind and very interested in anything one tells them. In the villages, a traveller will be given pineapples, bananas or sugar-cane to take on his journey. Nigeria is a very friendly land to travel in.

Markets

The markets are the shopping centres of Nigeria. The Nigerians love their markets and visit them not only to do their shopping but also to exchange gossip with friends or acquaintances and to hear all the news.

In nearly every large village and in all the towns there is a market. A large open space is set aside, and covered stalls are set up all the way round it.

A large, bustling market in the city of Kaduna

A smaller village market. Nigerians love their markets and come to them not only to buy and sell but also to meet their friends

Some markets are very large. One can buy almost anything there: a car or a camera; an electric generator or a top hat. Food, clothes and cosmetics are all on sale, and the goods come from all over the world: from Africa, America, Europe and Asia.

People ply their trade in the market—there are mechanics and tailors, and native doctors who sell medicines for various ailments. There are even people who offer their services as letter-writers to those who cannot read or write.

You need never go hungry or thirsty on market day. There are snack bars where you can eat fried locusts—or, if you prefer,

55

ice-cream—and drink palm-wine or beer or tea. And there are jugglers, dancers and musicians to entertain you.

All the merchants selling the same kind of goods group themselves together. There may be a long row of stalls where shoes are sold. Another section will offer clothing for sale. A very large area will be taken up by sellers of various foodstuffs. Each seller has a pile of food in front of him—a mound of pine-apples, a basketful of mangoes or a big sackful of maize. Often goods are not sold by weight, but are measured out in cigarette tins, or match-boxes or cups.

The carpenters, butchers, mechanics and barbers are men, but nearly all the other stall-holders are women. They are called "market mammies" and they are very good at their job. Many cannot read or write and they carry all their business in their heads. Some of them are very rich. They live in large houses, have their own servants and take holidays in Europe. These "market mammies" have been buying and selling things since they were children. Quite small girls in Nigeria can be seen selling food and fruit. They carry their goods on their heads in a basket or in a big wash-basin. By the time they are grown-up they know everything about the markets.

Buying and selling is done by bargaining. Two people may spend a long time haggling over the price, but once they reach agreement they accept one another's word. If a seller or buyer tried to cheat, he would be beaten and told never to come back.

As so many people go to the markets, it is here that important announcements are made—for instance, that children are to be vaccinated in a certain district or that the adult education teacher will visit a village on a certain day.

When Nigerians go to a market they often walk. If the market is a long way away they usually travel by public lorry. These lorries, which are sometimes very old, are called "mammy waggons". They travel all over the country carrying people and their goods. Most of them have a saying painted on them, such as *Better late than never*, or *Trust in God*. When these mammy waggons break down or get stuck in the rainy season, the passengers all get out and help.

Transport

Not many years ago, when somebody had to make a journey to a district where there was no road or railway, he had to walk. Food and other necessities had to be prepared and carefully packed. Then carriers had to be found. Each man carried a load on his head and the procession halted every afternoon, camping out and then packing up and moving on the next morning. Traders, officials, doctors, engineers and missionaries all travelled in this way. The journeys often took many days and were very expensive.

Nowadays, many stretches of road and railways have been laid, and travelling is no longer the difficult undertaking it once was.

The two most important roads in Nigeria both run from the west to the east. They are part of a network connecting West Africa with East Africa.

The railways have been laid in such a way that the two main ports—Lagos and Port Harcourt—are connected with the capital cities of the chief states. The first locomotives used wood for fuel. Later, coal was discovered near Enugu and this was used instead. Since then, oil has been found, and an increasing number of diesel trains have been put into service.

The waterways, too, are used for trade and travel. Boats can sail right up the River Niger to Jebba, and up the River Benue

A Nigerian water-bus. Where there are few roads and railways, the rivers are often used for getting from place to place

as far as Yola; and during the rainy season, they can go much further.

But perhaps the most useful form of transport in Nigeria is the aeroplane. All the main towns have an airport, and many smaller places have a landing-field which can be used by light aircraft. Now an engineer can go and examine a bridge and a doctor can treat a sick person very quickly. Nigerians like flying and they make good pilots.

Modern rail, road and river transport has helped the Nigerians in another way as well. It has made it possible for farmers and producers to work together and sell their produce jointly—that is, to co-operate. Near Kano, thousands of small farmers grow groundnuts on their little plots of land. At harvest time the farmers bring the nuts to the co-operative

59

society, which stores, transports and sells their produce for them. There are thousands of co-operative societies in Nigeria, all managed by Nigerians.

A very interesting co-operative society is the Community of the Apostles. In 1940, a few fishermen in a poor village in western Nigeria decided that they wanted a better life for their families, so they pooled their resources. Their source of income was fish, which they sold in Lagos. The money was kept by their treasurer and every family was given what it needed. The rest of the money was used to build better houses, schools, hospitals and nurseries. The poor muddy fishing village has now become a pleasant, healthy and prosperous town.

As the roads and railways reached out further, it became possible to take better care of the people. Doctors and nurses could travel to out-of-the-way places and explain to people how to avoid diseases. Mosquitoes and certain flies carry diseases like malaria, yellow fever, sleeping sickness and river-blindness, which make people so weak that they cannot work. Everywhere in Nigeria there are people now whose job it is to destroy these flies and mosquitoes.

Food

Nigerian people live very simply. They have one big—sometimes very big—meal in the afternoon, and a small one in the evening before they go to bed. Nearly all their food is home-grown and is prepared at home. Instead of plates or dishes, Nigerians use baskets of plaited straw, and they eat with their fingers.

Some food is quite easy to cultivate. In the wet, warm south they grow root vegetables such as yams, cocoyams and sweet potatoes. The yam is a tuberous plant like the potato. It has a black outer skin and is white inside. Yams can be boiled or mashed, just like potatoes.

In the drier parts of the country, much maize is grown. The maize is dried and ground, and the rough flour is made into a dough. This dough, which is called *foo-foo*, can be eaten on its own or with some kind of sauce.

Another popular food is *garri*. This is made from the roots of a shrub called the cassava. The roots are pounded in tall wooden mortars, and then boiled or fried.

Nigerians like rice and in the rainy parts of the country rice grows well. There is very little bread, because the climate is not suitable for wheat-growing.

Meat can be obtained in all the markets, but it is expensive and for this reason the Nigerians keep a lot of hens and ducks.

A girl selling fruit in a market in Ibadan

They also like goat-meat and antelope-meat, and the flesh of
hedgehogs and of giant water-snakes—both of which taste very
good.

In the north, where huge herds of cattle are kept, the Fulani
and Kanuri women make butter, but the people do not drink
much milk—in fact, most milk is imported in tins.

Much dried fish is brought into Nigeria from Europe. It

62

comes in big bundles looking like dry sticks of wood. Nigerians use this fish for soups or to make sauces for garri, foo-foo and yams.

Nigeria grows a great deal of fruit of all kinds. Bananas can be seen growing in almost every garden. There are paw-paws, delicious mangoes, and pineapples—which can also be found growing wild in forest clearings. Oranges, limes and grape-fruits grow in many orchards.

A less well-known crop, from which a very well-known drink is made, is the kola nut. The kola trees produce a fruit which looks like a green grapefruit. In due course, the green outer skin falls away, revealing the silver and pink nuts. Coca-cola is made from the juice of these nuts. Africans chew them when they are thirsty. If a Nigerian gives you a kola nut, it is a sign of friend-ship.

Sugar-cane can be bought in the markets, but many people grow it at home. The hard outer casing, which is peeled away, looks like green bamboo. The white inner fibres are juicy and sweet.

For cooking, Nigerians use oil. In the north, groundnut oil is used and in the south, palm oil.

Natural Resources

Nigeria grows thousands of tonnes of groundnuts—which we call peanuts—both for her own use and for sale abroad. The low groundnut plant has a tangle of shoots above the ground, the "nuts", which are actually seeds, forming underground. When they are ripe, the whole family helps to harvest them. The roots are pulled up and the nuts are dried in the sun. The oil which is pressed out of the nut is used for cooking and the rest of the nut is eaten as food.

Another kind of oil comes from the oil-palm. When we eat margarine or use soap, it is almost certain that the palm oil which they contain comes from Nigeria. This oil is the chief crop in the Eastern Region of the country.

The oil-palm likes a warm, wet climate. The tree grows straight up to a height of over nine metres (thirty feet) or more. There the leaves branch out. The fruit grows in bunches at the base of the leaves. Thousands of little oil-palm fruits make up one of these bunches, each bunch the size of a large football.

Each fruit consists of a hard nut covered by a softer shell. The oil which is pressed from the shell is called palm oil, and the oil

64

A harvest of groundnuts. The plants have been pulled up, and the "nuts", which grow under the ground, have now been laid out to dry in the sun

which is extracted from the nut is known as palm kernel oil.

After the bunches of fruit have been cut down, they are collected and taken in lorries to the oil-mill. On some very big plantations there is a small railway which takes the produce to the mills. The oil-mills are like factories and the biggest of them is at Port Harcourt.

65

In the mills, the single fruits are separated from the stems. Then the soft outer shell is separated from the hard kernel.

Big presses squeeze the palm oil out of the shells. The oil is cleaned and piped into storage tanks. Later it is piped direct to the docks and into waiting ships.

The palm kernel oil is used to make margarine, and the crushed and dried kernels are fed to milking-cows.

Bunches of oil-palm fruits; each little fruit has a soft outer shell and a hard inner nut, and oil is extracted from both shell and nut

Tapping a rubber tree

Country people in Nigeria have their own use for palm oil. When it starts to rain, instead of putting on a raincoat they take off their clothes. Then they smear their bodies with palm oil and the rain rolls off their oily skin. They say it is much better than having to go about in wet clothes.

Cocoa is grown in the Western and Mid-Western States. It is from the cocoa bean that chocolate is made. The cocoa beans grow inside a shell which is a little smaller than a rugby football.

Cocoa trees are difficult to grow. The seedlings like warmth, but they also like shade, so they are planted under other trees.

A young rubber plantation

A Nigerian tin mine

Much rubber is produced in Nigeria. The rubber trees grow
in plantations, many of them covering vast areas. When the
rubber is ready to be collected, a length of bark is cut off
round the trunk. Then a small cup is fastened to the trunk.
Where the bark has been cut the tree "bleeds" and a white

liquid called latex drips into the cup. The liquid is collected and smoked, and becomes the raw rubber.

Some of Nigeria's wealth, such as tin, is to be found below the ground. There are important mines in Benue-Plateau State. The miners direct strong jets of water into the hillsides. The earth crumbles and most of it is washed away. The heavy part —which holds the tin—remains and this is transported to the factories.

Nigeria also has columbite, a valuable substance used for making steel extra hard. With columbite better jet engines can be manufactured.

Everyone in Nigeria was glad when coal was discovered near Enugu in the East Central State. Although it is not as hard or as black as the best coal, it is still very useful to the country.

People were even more pleased when, after a long search, oil was found in the swampy eastern coastal area. There is enough oil for the whole of Nigeria, and a surplus besides which is exported to other countries. A large port was built at Bonny near the oilfields. It has a specially long jetty so that ships can come and fill up with oil which is pumped out through pipelines. Now there are four more oil terminals.

As time goes on, more and more oil is being found in Nigeria. The quality of this oil is excellent and it is being exported in large quantities, thus improving the country's economy.

Nigerian member of an oil-drilling crew at work

There is one substance, more important than all the others, which has been found under the ground; and that is water.

During the dry season many small rivers and streams disappear. Without water, animals die of thirst and nothing will grow. For many years the governments of Britain and Nigeria employed scientists to search for water. At last the experts discovered that if they bored a sufficiently deep hole in the earth, they would reach water. These very deep wells are called

The Bonny Tanker terminal. The jetty which can be seen in the picture is for the use of small craft only. The one for tankers goes much further out to sea

This picture of a water pumping-station scheme may appear ordinary but to the people of Nigeria it represents one of the miracles of modern scientific progress

"artesian wells", and they have saved many lives. There are now thousands of these wells in Nigeria and the government hopes that eventually every small village will have its own supply of water.

Education and Art

Nigerian children have to work very hard when they first go to school. At home with their families they speak their own tribal languages. At school, all the classes are held in English so they have to start learning what for them is a foreign language.

Some village schools are quite small and are built of wooden planks with a thatched roof. The floor is beaten clay or earth,

74

and there are long tables and benches for the pupils and a separate table and chair for the teacher. The same subjects are taught as in British schools, but learning takes longer because everything is taught in English.

In the larger towns, the schools are built of stone or cement, and many have sports-grounds. Nigerian schoolboys are very fond of all forms of games and sport.

After six years at primary school, the best pupils go on to grammar school. As there are not enough grammar schools, there is great competition for places. A school with a hundred places may have as many as a thousand students applying for admission. Most of these schools are boarding-schools because the students come from far away.

Lagos University

Outside a modern school building. Organized games are part of the school curriculum in Nigeria

Nigerians are so eager to learn that they do not always wait for the government or the missionaries to build a school. One of the best schools in Nigeria was started in this way. Some years ago, Tai Solarin—later a famous headmaster—took seventy boys with him to the bush near Ikenne in the Western State. They cleared the forest and built their own school. Five years later, they had built nearly forty more buildings, and there are now many hundreds of boys and girls attending the school.

Until 1948, a Nigerian student wishing to go to college had to go overseas, because there were no universities in Nigeria. But in 1948 the government of the colony of Nigeria founded the country's first university at Ibadan. The majority of the students train to be teachers, because in a country the size of Nigeria many teachers are needed.

By the time Nigeria became independent in 1960, one university was not sufficient. More and more teachers, and doctors and lawyers and engineers were needed. The first thing the government of independent Nigeria did was to open more universities. Throughout the country, there are now twenty-four, with over 90,000 students.

These young men have been given time off from work to study at this technical training school

There are many older Nigerians who have never been to school. They are now being given the opportunity of learning to read and write in English. Travelling teachers go round from village to village, and people come from far away to be taught.

Schools and universities have brought Western culture to Nigeria, but the people have had their own learning, art and culture for a very long time—long before the first Europeans came.

More than two thousand years ago, in the valley of the Benue river, lived a large tribe named Nok. Although they have disappeared, traces of their civilization can still be seen in the pieces of stone sculpture, pottery, tools and various implements which they left behind. Then, too, near the Cross river, hidden by the forest, there are monuments of stone, which were left by another tribe. Yoruba artists in Benin and Ife made beautiful objects and statues six hundred years ago. The bronze statues of Benin are very famous and so are the figures made of brass.

Where there was no bronze or brass or stone, artists turned to wood. Some trees in Nigeria, such as ebony or ironwood, are extremely hard and both in the east and west of the country artists carved figures in wood. There are many of these carvings in the museums of Europe and America and in the new museums of Africa.

In northern Nigeria, where timber is scarce, carving was done in ivory, and craftsmen also worked in silver or gold. The

Musicians with unusual instruments provide music and rhythm for dancers at Kaduna

Arab teachers who came to northern Nigeria left behind beautifully written and bound manuscripts. The northern people also built large mosques and made coloured tiles for walls and floors.

All Nigerians are fond of music. The music sounds a little strange to European ears because there is no obvious melody. The music is mostly for dancing to, and the main thing about it is the beat or rhythm. Not surprisingly the chief instrument in Nigerian music is the drum.

Usually, this is made from a hollowed-out log. Across the ends, pieces of fine goatskin are stretched, and between them vertical strands of thin cord are tightly tied, all the way round the drum. By pressing one or more of the cords with his arm, the drummer can produce different sounds. The drum is slung round the shoulder on a strap and is beaten with a short stick.

"Talking" drums are much larger and heavier and are placed on the ground. The ends are not covered and the sounds vary according to the hollowness, thickness and length of the log. These drums are used for sending messages in country districts where there is no telegraph or telephone.

Dances are part of every entertainment and celebration. Tribes, districts and villages all have their own traditional dances. Many of them are for men only. Sometimes they commemorate an event in the past of the tribe. The chief dancer may wear a huge mask and a disguise of feathers and grass. Some costumes are made up entirely of coloured beads. The steps vary from dance to dance but they all follow the beat of

A display of dancing, featuring a traditional war-dance. The dancers swiftly circle the warrior lying on the ground while the war-drum reaches fever-pitch

the drums, the dancers stamping, swaying and sometimes jumping into the air.

Nigerians enjoy dancing very much. Often a dance will start because somebody has returned home or has passed an examination successfully—or simply for the pleasure of dancing.

A Visit to a Small Village

The small villages of Nigeria are not on the main roads. The best way to reach them is by jeep or Land-Rover. Even so, it is often necessary to walk part of the way. The winding paths in the bush are not made for motor vehicles.

Here and there along the path are small clearings where yams or sweet potatoes or banana trees have been planted.

As you approach the village you pass small gardens. The village itself may be completely hidden by the forest until you arrive at the first house.

The houses are quite small and there may be several of them built close together and surrounded by a fence, making what is known as a compound. Some fences consist of spiky plants in a long row. Others are simply stakes driven into the ground and tied together with creepers. As the soil is warm and fertile, many of the stakes begin to sprout and grow leaves, flowers or even fruit.

There are no streets in the village, but paths lead from one compound to another.

The houses have no chimneys. Cooking is done inside, and the smoke simply escapes through the thatched roof. In the bigger villages, there is a school, a dispensary where medicines

A village "street" scene

are prepared, and sometimes a postal agency or depot. Once a week the postman comes to the depot to deliver and collect the mail. If the village is Christian, there will also be a small church or chapel.

The villagers keep a wide variety of animals: dogs, hens, ducks, black goats, black pigs and black sheep.

In the morning, as soon as it is light, everybody in the village is up and about. Girls carrying buckets on their heads can be seen going towards the nearest stream or well to fetch water.

The women begin their washing, or start preparing food. The men go off to their work on the land. Each carries a cutlass or matchete. These are heavy knives, about sixty centimetres (two feet) in length. They are used for a variety of jobs: to cut through the bush, to dig, to cut firewood, or to chop up meat.

Many of the women go to work in the vegetable gardens. They march off together, carrying their wide-bladed, short-handled hoes on their heads.

All country people go to bed when it becomes dark. For light, they use oil-lamps or hurricane-lamps, known as "bush lamps". In the larger villages there is a policeman and sometimes a guard for the night, who is known as the "watchnight".

The first thing a visitor does, on arrival in a village, is to go and greet the local chief. The headman—or chief—looks and dresses like the other villagers, but he carries a carved or decorated staff.

Visitors are invited into the chief's compound because, like all Nigerians, the headman is pleased to see strangers. He also likes to offer drink and food. The drink may be corn beer made of maize or palm wine from oil-palm trees. The chief usually has his own ceremonial drinking horn and the beer or wine is poured out of a calabash. This is a dried pumpkin with a long, curved neck at one end. Some types of calabash are quite big and are decorated with designs or with beadwork or strips of coloured leather.

Inside the house there is very little furniture, but every headman or chief has his stool. It is made from the trunk of a tree and decorated with carvings, representing animals—the leopard is a common choice—or human figures. The visitors are offered a simple chair or stool to sit on. But nobody sits down or speaks unless he is first invited to by his host.

The village chief is a very important man in Nigeria. He knows everybody and he is the link between the government and the people.

When he has to make a major decision, he asks his friends in the village to come and talk the matter over with him. The village may need a new school, or the people may want a better road. The matter is discussed by the village council. Sometimes, the council will meet in the open, with everyone sitting under a big, shady tree. When the question has been settled, the chief goes to a government official in the nearest big town and speaks for his people.

Villagers like to form themselves into clubs or societies. Men and women of more or less the same age form groups to help one another. If one member has a son who is a promising student, his club or society will lend him money to pay for further studies. The money will be repaid to the society once the student starts earning.

Most villagers earn their living by farming. If the village is a long way from the main road, the men take their produce to the nearest big village where there is a market. In the market their produce is bought by a trader who transports it to the towns. Sometimes the farmers do not sell their goods for money, but exchange them for something they need. This is called "barter-trade".

Until the European traders came, the Nigerians did not buy and sell things for money. In the southern part of Nigeria, cowrie shells were used as money. In the north, the cattle-owning tribes counted their wealth in cattle: the more cattle a man owned, the richer he was. Gold and silver were recognized as valuable, but were not used for money, and paper money was unsuitable because the people could not read and could not therefore understand what the different banknotes signi-

Factory skills are being learned by the people of Nigeria. This picture shows the production of polythene bags

fied. There are remote places in Nigeria where even now the people do not like paper money and prefer to use coins.

Many young men leave the villages to work on plantations or in factories in the towns, where they can make more money. Although they often visit their homes, once they have lived in a large town many of them do not wish to return to live in their villages any more.

Nigeria's Place in Africa

When, in 1960, independence came to Nigeria, the Queen of England became the Queen of independent Nigeria. But many Nigerians felt that it was not right for a strange ruler, living far away, to be the head of their country. So they decided to turn Nigeria into a republic and to have a president of their own. But, at the same time, they chose to remain a member of the Commonwealth.

Because the British governed the country for so many years, they have had much influence on the way the country is run. The police force, for example, follows the British pattern, and the legal system is based on that of England.

Nevertheless, some laws which work well in Britain do not always work in Nigeria. And there are also many tribal laws and customs which the people have followed for centuries and which are important to them. So the country has two separate kinds of law which work side by side; there are the laws made by the government of Nigeria and those of the tribes.

Since her independence, Nigeria has become a very good example to other African countries. She has learned from the Europeans and uses this knowledge intelligently. To begin with, she has shown how important it is to educate people. More children go to school in Nigeria than in any other African country. Then, too, she has learned how to overcome many of the tropical diseases; and, where diseases such as leprosy do still occur, the government—that is, the whole country—cares for the sick people.

Other African countries have, in recent years, sent their people to Nigeria to see how she manages her affairs, and Nigeria sends her teachers and professors to advise other countries on how to run their schools and universities. In addition, many lawyers, architects, doctors, nurses and engineers have been sent by Nigeria to other African countries.

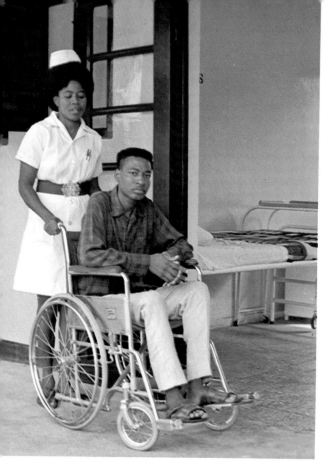

Nigeria ia a member of the World Health Organization. She is conscious of the need for facilities like those shown here—in a modern hospital

In 1963, Nigeria decided to become part of the Organization of African States. The countries belonging to this organization work to create a better life for all Africans.

In a country as huge as Nigeria, where so many millions of people live, it takes time to improve the general standard of living. Nigeria has been independent for a very few years, and her way of life is changing all the time. There is not enough money to pay for all the improvements which are needed, so Nigeria has to rely on help from other countries.

Much of this help is given by the United Nations which is an association of all the countries of the world. This association has established special groups giving technical aid. One group helps farmers to grow better crops and to breed healthier animals. Another group advises on education and improved living conditions. Then there is the World Health Organization which tries to ensure that the people lead healthier lives. Nigeria herself is a member of these groups and she, in her turn, helps other countries as much as she can.

The Supreme Court Lagos—one example of Nigeria's efforts to establish the rule of a just law at the time of independence

Aid comes from other directions as well. There are teachers from the United States and Britain, and missionaries from Ireland; there are Dutch farming experts and many others.

One hundred years ago, Nigeria was an enormous stretch of land inhabited by many different tribes who were kept in order by a foreign government.

Recently, she has become a flourishing country belonging to a prosperous and healthy people. Unfortunately, however, bitter strife between the Federal Government of Nigeria and the breakaway state of Biafra threatened the country's security and progress. Those threats were successfully overcome, but others still exist. And, while they do, the future must remain uncertain. However, there can be no doubt that Nigeria has secured for herself a well-deserved position among the countries of modern Africa.

Index